How to End the Worry Habit

By Bernadette M. Farrell

How to End the Worry Habit

PUBLISHED BY

Bernadette M. Farrell at Amazon

How to End the Worry Habit

Copyright © 2011 by Bernadette M. Farrell

Acknowledgements

Inspiration for this book has come from many sources, including the numerous people I have worked with down through the years, who showed a willingness to learn new ways of doing, thinking and seeing the world.

CONTENTS

There is nothing either good or bad,

but thinking makes it so.

— William Shakespeare

A Training Session in Boston

Ann-Marie O'Donnell sat quietly in Room 121. The only sound was the ticking of the large clock on the wall. Time passed slowly as she waited for the participants to filter in. It was day two of the training program: *Dealing with Worry and Anxiety in your Work and in your Life*.

Worry and Anxiety were big issues in people's lives. Ann-Marie knew this to be the case. A recent look at Google's records had shown her that 673,000 searches per month had been made using the word "Worry". For "Anxiety" the figure was even higher: 2,740,000 monthly searches had been made. The figures had not surprised Ann-Marie. She knew from her own experience that there were a lot of people who needed help in overcoming worry and the anxiety that it creates. She also knew that people made rapid progress in putting an end to their own particular worries and anxieties, when they were shown how.

This was the reason that she had decided to organize the training session. She wanted to show people, that overcoming the worry habit was something that could be achieved, without too much difficulty. Because she wanted to make the learning process as painless as possible, she had decided that she would give participants a short story to read, prior to coming on the program. The story would provide them with the tools that they needed to overcome worry and anxiety in their own lives.

The story she had given them was the tale of two characters called Little Brave and Little Worrier. Little Brave was optimistic and ever ready for a challenge. His friend, Little Worrier was full of fear and always imagined that the worst was going to happen. When a storm came and destroyed their island home, Little Worrier was forced to make a journey. During the course of the journey, he learned how to change his way of thinking, so that he no longer worried and made life hard for himself.

The message of the story was simple, yet profound and was just what was needed, Ann-Marie believed, to show people how they could release themselves from the pain and suffering of worry and anxiety in their own lives.

The first training session had taken place two months earlier. In that first session, the group had looked at the obstacles faced by Little Brave as he made his journey to the other side of the island.

Today, they were going to be discussing Little Worrier and how he had managed to overcome his fears and anxieties about the future. The group would have the opportunity to talk about the lessons they had learned from his story and to relate how they themselves had applied those lessons, to overcome worries and anxieties within themselves and within their own organizations.

As the group waited for latecomers to arrive, they spent the time catching up on the events that had happened in each other's lives, since their last meeting.

"I believe that congratulations are in order," Doug said, as Bill walked into the room.

"Yes, we had a little girl. She has Laura's good looks," Bill said.

"I am glad that she doesn't have yours," Doug added. The good natured banter between the two was alive and well.

Eventually, the talk turned to the subject of the day's training session.

"I went through a bad time with worry about six months ago," Josh said, "I was wakening in the morning with tightness across my chest. 'What if it's my heart?'

'What if I'm going to die?' "I believed that there was something seriously wrong with me. Nothing could convince me otherwise. I had been to see my G.P. She had assured me that everything was fine. I had gone to see her more than once. She had even sent me for tests at the hospital. They were all clear. But I couldn't get it out of my head. At work, I couldn't concentrate. Every time I got the tight feeling, I thought I was going to drop down dead. My anxiety levels were at an all-time high. If it wasn't for that little book, I don't know how I would have coped.

"That's good to hear Josh, I am glad that you found the book helpful," Anne-Marie said. "I am looking forward to hearing more from you later.

"I started having panic attacks while driving, Julie said. I was seriously worried that my car was going to go out of control. I thought that at any moment, it would just veer off the road and hit the barrier or swerve into the inner lane and hit another vehicle. I'd had to give up driving altogether. When I read Little Worrier's story, it made so much sense to me. I am back driving now and thankfully my panic attacks are a thing of the past.

"Maybe you would like to share with us later, what it was that you did, to put an end to your panic," Anne-Marie said.

"Yes, I would be more than happy to do that," Julie added.

"I have been so busy with work, that I haven't had a chance to read my copy of Little Worrier's story," Jen said. "I am working on a project at the moment that has been stressing me out. I am worried that I won't meet my deadline and that my work won't meet with my boss's high standards. I am not sleeping well. I can't 'switch off', even at week-ends."

"Jen, I think that you will benefit a lot from hearing what Little Worrier has to say about how he overcame the worry habit," Bill said.

"I am glad to hear you say that Bill," Abe added. "We have a lot of people, who do the 'worry thing' in my organization. They can be very hard to work with when you are trying to bring in change." Abe was one of the people who hadn't been able to attend the previous session and hadn't yet had an opportunity to read Little Worrier's story.

"Yeah, I know what you are talking about," Bill said, "We had lots of worriers in our organization – people who were fearful of change. We needed to bring them with us. We managed to do this, but only when we took the time to listen to their fears – their 'what ifs.' To be truthful, we hadn't made the connection between their resistance and their 'what ifs.' We used Little Worrier's story to bring the subject out into the open."

"I have often wondered what happens to the worriers of this world – the ones who are fearful of change," Abe said.

"Hopefully, together we will be able to shed some light on your question Abe, about what happens to the worriers of this world," Ann-Marie said. "So without any further delay, let's just remind ourselves of Little Worrier's story." Ann Marie added "Who would like to start the ball rolling, by telling the story in his or her, own words?"

"I'll give it a go," Bill said.

"Good man Bill, just don't take the scenic route, we would all like to get home before the sun comes up in the morning," Doug added.

"Don't worry Doug I will be short and sweet. I wouldn't like to be responsible for depriving you of your beauty sleep." And so Bill began to tell the tale of Little Brave and Little Worrier and how Little Worrier managed to overcome his worries and anxieties, so that he was able to make the journey to the other side of the island.

Life on the Island

The two friends spent their days tending their small vegetable plots or herding the sheep and goats that roamed freely on the mountainside. Sometimes, they liked to sit on the rocks at the water's edge and to catch the brightly colored fish that were in abundant supply. In the late afternoon, when their day's work was done, they went swimming or snorkeling in the clear blue sea that surrounded the island.

Little Brave was hopeful and always up for a challenge. He liked to swim so far out to sea that he couldn't be seen from the shoreline, and when he went diving, he enjoyed pushing himself beyond his limits, bringing back shells and pieces of coral, that no-one had ever seen before.

His friend, Little Worrier was more cautious and had the habit of always thinking, that the worst was going to happen. When Little Brave called to him to swim further out to sea, he would immediately think, "What if a big wave comes and pulls me under?" Being able to 'see' the worst happening in his mind's eye ensured that he stayed safe and close to the shoreline. He applied this way of seeing things, to everything that he did. When one of the goats or sheep went missing, the first thought in his head was "What if it's been attacked, what if it's been eaten by a wild beast?" Any time he got an ache or a pain, he couldn't stop himself from thinking "What if I am ill – really ill? What if I never recover?" When he heard about something awful happening to someone else, he would think "What if it happens to me?" When he was told that visitors were coming to the island, his immediate thought was, "What if they don't like me? What if they prefer Little Brave to me?" This kind of thinking meant that he lived in a constant state of worry and apprehension. He didn't realize that he was thinking in this worrisome way – it had become such a habit, that he wasn't aware that he was doing it.

Even though he lived on the most beautiful island imaginable, his way of thinking clouded and colored his view, making even the most idyllic way of life fraught with insecurity and doubt.

The Storm

One night, a storm hit the island. It had been the worst in living memory. The wind howled and hollered, lifting everything in its path. Trees and plants were ripped from their roots. The very soil that had given them sustenance was torn away, leaving only barren rock in its place. The sea had risen several feet into the air and had swept across the island. For three days, the storm raged. The sheep and goats, unable to withstand the force of the wind were carried over the cliff's edge and into the sea. Fish, once plentiful in the waters around the island, had all but disappeared.

The two friends, who were huddled together in their cave high up in the mountains, watched in disbelief as their beloved landscape was ravaged and ruined. The hearts in their little chests beat so wildly, that it felt like at any moment, they would surely burst. Beads of perspiration dropped from their brows, as fear gripped every fiber of their being.

When the storm had finally abated, they were faced with such incredible devastation that they could hardly believe their eyes. "What the hell are we going to do now?" Little Worrier, close to tears, asked his friend. "Everything is destroyed. It's all gone. It's all that stuff that they have been putting into the atmosphere – that's what's caused this problem. It's their fault. I'll get to the bottom of this – I'll figure out what's really been happening here."

"It is nature's way," Little Brave said in a hushed voice. "These things happen. We need to go and see what's on the other side of the island. The storm probably didn't hit that side as badly as it hit us here."

"It's a long way off. We'd have to find our way across the mountain. Anything could happen to us out there. What if we don't find our way? What if we are attacked and left for dead? Things will probably pick up here after a while. Why should we have to go? We haven't done anything wrong. Somebody will probably come along and help us out, if we wait. I think we should wait and see what happens."

Because he didn't want to leave his friend, Little Brave decided to stay. Each day they took it in turns to go to the water's edge, to see if there was any help on the horizon, each day they returned with their spirits lower than the day before.

One day, Little Brave decided that he had had enough. It wasn't in his nature to sit around and wait for things to change. He tried once more to convince his friend, that they needed to take action, but Little Worrier wasn't having any of it.

"You go if you want to. This is my home. I have never lived anywhere else. I'm not leaving."

"The storm has cleared everything away – there's nothing left here for us now," Little Brave reasoned. "Things will grow again at some-time in the future – that's how nature works, but for now we have to accept what's happened. We need to move with the changes."

But Little Worrier wasn't listening any more – he had walked away.

The next morning, Little Brave packed a bag and as he slung it over his shoulder, he made his way toward the trail that would eventually lead to the other side of the island. Little Worrier had a knot in his stomach as he bade farewell to his friend, fearful that he might never see him again.

The Other Side of the Island

At first, Little Brave found the going very tough. Much of the terrain was rough and unyielding. He had faced many obstacles along the way – facing them alone had been particularly difficult. He missed the company of the friend that he had left behind. However, despite the trials and tribulations that he met, he had managed to arrive safely at the other side of the island.

He had learned many lessons along the way and was happy now to be settling into life in a new place. He had seen many things that he had never seen before – buildings that reached high into the sky, exciting places to eat and drink, exotic food that he had never tasted in the past, a harbor that stretched far out into the sea, with a jetty that housed boats and yachts with sails, the size of which he had never even dreamed about.

He thought often about Little Worrier and wondered not for the first time, how he might be coping. As he made his way, one afternoon, for a swim, he saw someone that looked familiar, coming in the distance. He wondered could it be his friend. As he came closer to him, he realized that it was indeed his friend – he had made the journey to the other side of the island after all. He was overjoyed to see him. After the two embraced, Little Worrier set about telling him, in his own words, how he had managed to overcome his fears and how he had succeeded in making the journey, to the other side of the island.

Little Worrier's Story

The Center for Alterations and Repairs

"When you left I was very, very angry. I was annoyed with you, for going off and leaving me on my own. I was thinking, some friend you turned out to be. The fact that you were able to do what I couldn't do – to face your fears and to go out into the unknown like that, made me feel even worse. I was beginning to feel hopeless. When I went to bed, I couldn't sleep. My mind was racing. Every thought in my head was negative: 'What if help doesn't come? What if I follow in your footsteps and I get lost or beaten up?' I couldn't switch off. I had to drag myself out of bed in the morning.

"One day I said to myself, 'I just can't keep going on like this. If I don't get some sleep, I will never be able to sort this out.' I decided to go and see the man who has a pill for every ill. When I told him my story, he took a pen and wrote on his notepad. When he finished he folded the paper in two and handed it to me.

"When I got outside, I opened the folded notepaper. It read 'Go to the Center for Alterations and Repairs.' I wondered had the world gone barking mad. 'Here I am worried. I can't sleep and I am being sent to have my clothes altered.' I looked down at my trousers. As far as I could make out, they were neither too long nor too short. I then checked my sleeves; again they seemed to be just the right length. When I put my thumb inside the waistband of my trousers, I noticed that it was indeed a little loose, but that wasn't too surprising – I had been too worried to even think about food.

"As this center place didn't look like it was too far away, I decided that it wouldn't do me any harm to go and have a look. I thought that I could get there by mid-day, if I went straight away.

"The Center for Alterations and Repairs was in an unusual building; when observed from one angle, the building looked one particular way, but when viewed from a different angle, it took on a different appearance altogether. Depending on the way that you looked at it, the color of the building also changed – sometimes it was black and white, at other times it was different shades of grey. It was in a part of the island that I had been to before, yet I had passed it by and never saw it.

"It was not a center for the alteration and repair of clothes, as I had first thought. It was in fact, a center for the alteration and repair of thinking conditions or habits – thinking habits like 'what-if-itis'. Now you know Little Brave, that when I was younger, I was unfortunate enough to have had a very nasty dose of tonsillitis, but I had never before even heard of a condition called 'what-if-itis'. This was a center for the repair of this condition. I knew this to be the case, for it said so in bold letters on a plaque over the door.

"I was hopping mad. 'Why have I been sent to this place? I don't have this condition or habit or whatever they call it. What if I can't find my way out of here? What if I don't get home before nightfall? It will be his fault. He obviously doesn't like me; that's why he has sent me here. I should have stayed where I was. What am I going to do now?"

Encounter with a 'Weismann'

"Just as I was about to turn on my heels and walk away, I noticed an imposing looking individual, peering in my direction. He had an air of authority about him, as though he knew a thing or two, but when he approached me, I was kind of surprised, because his greeting was warm and friendly. He introduced himself as W.J. Weismann. He said 'You look very worried, what's up?'

"I told him, 'I've been sent to this place and I don't know why I've been sent.'

"He listened to what I was saying and because he seemed interested, I ended up telling him the whole story about how the storm had come and destroyed everything and how you had gone off to the other side of the island and I had been left on my own.

"He asked me 'What is it that worries you most about the situation?'"

"'I need to go to the other side of the island,' I said 'and I am worried about getting lost. What if I go out there and lose my way?'"

"'So, your biggest worry or your biggest fear is that you will get lost – is that it?'"

"'Yes, that's right,' I said. 'I could very easily get lost. People get lost all the time, you know. What if it happens to me?'

"I told him the story that I'd heard as a child. You probably heard it too, about a man who headed out on a journey and was never heard from again."

"Oh yeah, I remember that story," Little Brave said.

"Well, I could imagine it happening to me. I told him that I could see it very clearly in my mind's eye. 'I have been walking all day. Night has fallen. I can't see more than an inch in front of me. I can hear strange sounds in the distance. I am alone and I am lost.'

"I said to him that it made me shiver, every time I thought about it and that I believed, that I would need to be mad, to venture out into the unknown like that."

"So, your biggest fear is that you will get lost and never be heard from again, is that right?' This Weismann guy asked me."

"Yes,' I said 'that's it exactly.'"

"And having this fear is stopping you from going out, from moving forward?'"

"Yes it is,' I said."

"Well it would, wouldn't it,' he said, 'that's what fear can do – it's the biggest obstacle to change that we face."

"I felt better after he said that – I knew that he got it – I knew that he understood what I was talking about.

"Then he said 'What can you do about it now? What can you do about the fear?'"

"I don't know what to do' I said. 'Trying to figure out what to do, is keeping me awake at night.'

"I told him that fear had been a constant companion to me all of my life. If I hadn't been afraid, then my life might have been very different.

"He then made a very odd suggestion to me. He said he thought it might be a good idea for me to go and visit the center's courtroom. Even though this made no sense to me at all, I decided to follow his advice."

"Now that's not like you at all, Little Brave said. You don't usually do what other people tell you to do. When I think of all of the times that I have tried to convince you to do something or other and you wouldn't hear of it,"

"Yeah, you are right. I know that I am not good at taking advice. But this Weismann individual had something about him – something that said that it was OK for me to trust him. He seemed to know what he was talking about and he really did seem to be concerned about me.

"The courtroom was on the second floor of the building. I took the lift. It was a circular room with a dome shaped roof. It was not like any courtroom, I had ever seen before. It was true that there was a judge, a jury and two lawyers. But instead of criminal and civil cases being heard, people were putting their 'what ifs' on trial."

"Putting their 'what's' on trial?" Little Brave asked.

"Their 'what ifs' – their fears – what if this happens, what if that happens, what if disaster strikes – that kind of thing.

"A middle aged person approached the bench, as I walked into the room. He said that he had a 'should' that he wanted to put on trial. The presiding judge, very kindly advised him, that 'shoulds' were listed for later: 'Please see the notice at the door.'

"The way that this court worked, was that the judge started off by talking people through what was going to happen.

"'Before you there are two lawyers – one lawyer for the Prosecution and one for the Defense,' he said. 'The Prosecution Lawyer must bring in evidence to prove the case – to prove what is on trial – to prove that your 'what if' is true."

"It struck me that when he said the word **must** he really meant what he said.

"He continued, 'To be admissible, any evidence brought into this courtroom must be backed up by facts.' Again you were left in no doubt, that when he said **must**, he meant **must**."

"'Then it will be the turn of the Defense Lawyer. It is his job to bring in evidence to show that what is on trial is not true. Again, this evidence **must** be backed up by facts. It will then be the job of the Judge and Jury to reach a verdict – based on the evidence before them. Is this person's 'what if' true or is it false?'"

"He then asked 'Does everybody understand the procedure?'

"I nodded my head in agreement.

"Before long, it was my turn to put my 'what if' on trial. My biggest fear was that I would get lost and never be heard from again. As I believed, that it was highly likely that this would happen, I felt a bit silly going before the judge and jury. But as I was already there, I thought that I might as well go ahead with it.

"The Prosecution Lawyer was the first to bring in evidence. He said, 'Little Worrier, have you ever been lost before?'

"'Yes I have,' I said, 'I have gotten lost before.'"

"'How many times have you been lost?'"

"'Twice – no three times,' I replied."

"'You have been lost three times?'"

"'Yes, that's correct and I know of a man who lost his way and was never heard from again,' I said."

"'Objection your honor,' the Defense Lawyer was on his feet. 'What's on trial is that Little Worrier will get lost. This is about him. Not about other people.'"

"'Objection sustained,' the Judge said."

"The Defense Lawyer then asked me, 'Little Worrier, what did you do when you got lost before?'"

"'Let me think — what did I do? What I did was — I retraced my steps back to where I started,' I said."

"'Even though you got lost, you were able to find your way back. Is that correct?'"

"'Yes it is.'"

"'How many times have you been out on the trail?'"

"'Thousands I suppose.'"

"'And out of those thousands you got lost three times. Is that right?'"

"'Yes I suppose it is.'"

"The Defense Lawyer took a pen and drew a circle. 'This circle represents all of the times you have been out on the trail. I would like you to put a mark on the circle that represents the number of times you have been lost.'"

"I took the pen and put a mark. It was just a dot. Compared to the rest of the circle it was very tiny.

"The lawyer asked, 'What do you think?'"

"I had to admit, that the number of times that I got lost, was so small, that it was hardly visible. The times when I hadn't gotten lost, were far greater than those times when I had. This came as a surprise to me."

"'Did anyone else that you know lose their way on the trail?'"

"'Well yes, Little Brave lost his way several times, but he too was able to find his way back.'"

"'So if the worst happens and you get lost, will you be able to do something about it?'"

"'Yes I will,' I said."

"'Will you get lost and never be heard from again?'"

"'No, I don't believe that I will.'

"I was beginning to get the picture. When I thought about going out onto the trail, I had thought about the worst thing that could happen. I had focused on that. I had come to believe that, that was real – that, that was definitely what was going to happen to me. I hadn't been able to see the bigger picture. I had ignored the fact that I had found my way back, when I was lost in the past and that you had done the same. I had also ignored the fact, that of the thousands of times I had been out on the trail, I had lost my way only three times.

"I was more capable than I had thought that I was. 'I like this way of looking at things,' I said to myself. 'It makes sense.'"

"'What conclusion do you believe that the Judge and Jury will come to?' the Defense Lawyer then asked me."

"'I believe that they will say, that it is far more likely than not, that I won't get lost and if I do get lost, then I will be able to do something about it.'

"I felt like skipping out of the courtroom. I felt so much freer and lighter than when I came in.

"To ensure that I would not forget this very important lesson, I wrote in my little notebook:

When you are Worried and Afraid – Put your 'What Ifs' on Trial"

Little Worrier's Journey
Ready to Go

"It was Wednesday. I got up early. I had been at the Center for Alterations and Repairs for two days. I was now ready to set out on my journey. I had put all of my fearful predictions on trial. It hadn't taken very long. In each case, the Judge and Jury had found in favor of the Defense and my 'what ifs' had been thrown out of court. Even though, they had seemed very real to me at the time, I had discovered, that there was in fact little or no basis for them out in the real world. This realization had come as a surprise and as a great relief to me.

"I had removed the smokescreen that had been covering my eyes. I was now able to see reality as it was. The storm had come and had cleared everything in its path. I needed to get moving. You had managed to move on – you had gone ahead of me. I had taken longer than you had and was paying a price, but at least I was ready to go now – well almost ready. I just had one more hurdle to get over then I would be on my way.

"Every time I had put my foot on the trail that led to the other side of the island, my heart had started to race. My breathing sped up. My legs had trembled uncontrollably. I felt dizzy and light headed. The sensations that I was feeling, had not only made me abandon my earlier attempts to make the journey, but had also started to trouble me in a way that was very worrying. I had begun thinking, 'What if those sensations mean that there is something seriously wrong with me?'

"As I set off on the trail, I started to feel those same sensations again; my breathing sped up, my legs trembled. I felt lightheaded and dizzy. However, unlike before, I now knew what I needed to do put an end to them. While I was at the center, I had been shown a neat little trick that would help to calm me down, any time I felt dizzy or light-headed. It involved cupping my hands and placing them over my nose and mouth and taking some nice easy breaths, in and out – no big gulps. I decided to give it a try. It took less than a minute and just as I had been shown, the dizzy feelings had disappeared."

"At the Center for Alterations and Repairs, I had taken the tour inside the model of the person's brain and had seen for myself, how change and the fears associated with it could set off the fear response; trembling and racing heart etc. Now I understood the reason that I had felt those fear sensations in the first place. By starting out on the trail to the other side of the island, I had done something that I hadn't done before – something that I believed was putting my life in danger: I had feared that I would be lost and never be heard from again. And because my brain believed that I was in danger, it had responded by increasing my breathing rate and my heart rate – it was in effect doing what it had been designed to do and that was to prepare me to fight or to run away. Inside the brain, I could see all the connections and how one could set off a reaction in the other.

"But why was I still having the anxious feelings – that's the bit that I didn't understand. I had put my fears about being lost and never being heard from again on trial and had discovered that my fears were unfounded – there was no evidence for them out in the real world. I no longer believed that going out on the trail posed a threat to my wellbeing. I knew that I was no longer in danger and my brain knew it too, so there was no need for it to set off my fight or flight response, yet this is exactly what had happened as soon as I started out on my journey. There were parts of this puzzle that I had not yet figured out.

"While I was inside the brain, I had seen that once the fear response had been triggered in a particular situation, the memory parts of the brain, recorded not only the place where that had happened, but also the actual feelings of fear themselves – the racing heart and trembling. Because a link had been made between the location and the feelings, all it took to trigger those sensations again, was a return visit to the original location or situation. Maybe this was the reason that I continued to feel anxious – by setting off on the trail again, I had also set off my recorded fear responses.

"Or it might have had to do with the fact that I was worried, that having those kinds of fear responses, meant that there was something seriously wrong with me and that it was the worry itself – the 'what if' about my physical well-being – my racing heart etc., that was actually causing the sensations that I was feeling. This is the way that my 'what if' thinking worked. I would start to become aware of the beating of my heart then I would say to myself, 'You know what, I think that my heart is beating faster than usual. What if this means that there is something wrong with me,' which in turn would make my heart beat even faster, which would convince me even further that there was something wrong with me. By the time I was done thinking in this way, my heart would be banging away in my chest and I would be convinced that I was in serious trouble. Thinking in this worrisome 'what if' way, was actually causing the very sensations that I dreaded so much. But hey you know what – even if this was what was happening, I wasn't too concerned, because now I had another trick up my sleeve.

"I now used the kind of approach that the lawyers had used with me in the courtroom. I asked myself, had it done me any harm in the past, when I felt those fear sensations – palpitations, trembling etc.? I thought back to all those times when my heart had beaten wildly and my body had been shaking. There was no evidence at all that these experiences had affected me in a harmful way. I had been checked out by the man who has a pill for every ill and had been given a clean bill of health. The Prosecution Lawyer didn't have one shred of evidence to support the case. 'If the physical sensations didn't harm me then, why would they do so now?' I asked myself. And because I no longer believed that they were in any way dangerous, I decided that I would just accept the feelings. I would go with them and see what happened.

"When I'd taken my tour of the brain, I had seen how acceptance of the anxious feelings had triggered the safety response – the response that would over-ride the fear response. Now it was as if my own brain had got the message that I was okay, because after a little while my heart wasn't racing anymore and my legs had stopped shaking. I could hardly believe it. I had found a way to overcome my fearful feelings. By simply accepting these sensations, I had gained control over them. I was ecstatic. I was reminded of a quote that I had seen on the wall at the Center for Alterations and Repairs. 'The experience of overcoming fear is extraordinarily delightful (Bertrand Russell).' It was true. I now had first-hand experience of it for myself.

"So that I would not forget the lesson, I wrote a reminder for myself:

Acceptance of Fearful Sensations Puts an End to Them"

How Imagination Fuels Anxiety

"I had enjoyed the tour of the model of the brain. The part that I had enjoyed the most and that I had found the most fascinating, was going inside the person's imagination.

"Kal's imagination was like a big movie screen. The production was in vivid color – bright blues, greens, yellows and a brighter orange than I had ever seen before. Some of the movies were short and funny. Others were old and had some bits missing. Some were sad and had unhappy endings. A lot of the movies were about the future. Those were the most frightening movies of all. I started to notice that the dialogue in those movies often started with 'What if?' 'What if I can't handle it? What if there's not enough? What if she leaves?' As the movie progressed, the scenes became darker and more frightening. Kal was in charge of the movie – he was the director. He was also the producer, the scriptwriter, the locations manager and the special effects person.

"But what I couldn't understand was why he would create such a movie – when it was clear that what he was doing was frightening himself, why would he do that?

"But wasn't this exactly what I myself had been doing? Hadn't I been frightening myself in exactly the same way? I had created a movie about what would happen when I went out onto the trail to find my way to the other side of the island, and the movie that I created was a horror movie. I could see myself getting lost and being set upon by thieves and vagabonds and being left for dead in a lonely and isolated place.

"It was starting to dawn on me, that I too had been using my imagination to frighten myself. The images – the fearful images that I put up on the screen in my imagination were mine – they were my own creation – no one else's. I was beginning to see that I was the cause of my own fear. I was doing this to me.

"I had also found it fascinating that when Kal started to think fearful 'what if' type thoughts and to imagine the worst, that this had a knock on effect in his body. As the frightening scenes came up on the screen in his imagination, I could see that his breathing had sped up and had become more erratic. As he continued to think in this fearful way, something else very strange happened – his breathing rate became fixed at a higher level. In other words he was now breathing more rapidly on an ongoing basis. Then something happened that was completely 'out of the blue'. He began to have panic-like sensations: He became dizzy and lightheaded. He started shaking and trembling. His heart was pounding in his chest. He felt faint and feared that he might fall over. He had a sensation of numbness down his arm and tingling around his mouth. He had shortness of breath. He was hot one minute and cold the next. It was very frightening to watch.

"I wondered did he also have a weird feeling that he was separate from himself, as though he was looking in on himself. This was exactly how I had felt after you left. I hadn't made the connection between thinking the frightening thoughts and the strange sensations that I was feeling. But I could see it all clearly now. I had thought at the time, that maybe I was losing my mind. I had come close to tears as I remembered that – it had been very, very frightening."

"But you are alright now, that's the main thing. You managed to get here, all safe and sound," Little Brave said.

"Yes I did and I am very glad to be here – knowing what I know now; those feelings will never have the same effect on me again, ever."

The Causes of Panic

"While I was inside the brain, I could see exactly how Kal's panic feelings had been triggered; they were not as random or as 'out of the blue' as they had first appeared."

"How do you mean?" Little Brave asked.

"Let me explain. Once Kal's breathing rate had been set at the new faster level, it had continued at this new level. With the increase in his breathing, there was also a change in the way that the blood was circulating in his brain; his blood vessels had in fact started to narrow. As his blood vessels narrowed, the supply of oxygen being carried in his blood to the different parts of his brain had slowed down; lowered blood supply meant that lowered amounts of oxygen were getting through. Then I noticed something else very strange – instead of releasing the oxygen to where it was needed in his brain, his blood was now holding onto much of the oxygen. As a consequence, his brain was now becoming starved of oxygen. It was at this point, I noticed that he had started to feel dizzy, lightheaded and faint. The numbness down his arm and tingling around his mouth had also kicked in. He had also started to feel like he was separate from himself – like he was looking in on himself. This made sense. His brain needed oxygen to function. When it was deprived of oxygen it had created those strange sensations."

"Wow, that's really incredible," Little Brave said. "It was his breathing that was causing all those weird sensations that he was feeling."

"Yes it was, but don't forget that it was his thinking that set off his breathing and his panic. It was when he started to think in the fearful 'what if' type way that his breathing got faster and more erratic. When his breathing got stuck at the higher level, his brain became deprived of oxygen and he began to feel dizzy and light headed and to get all those other weird sensations."

Overcoming Sensations of Panic

"But what really amazed me was when Kal began to breathe into his cupped hands – to breathe back in the air that he had breathed out, the blood vessels actually opened up, allowing the blood to flow again more freely. In addition, the oxygen was now being released to his brain where it was needed. With the increase in oxygen supply, I could see that his dizziness and other weird sensations had disappeared. What I witnessed had had such an impact on me that I couldn't wait to try out this re-breathing thing for myself.

"As the panic kicked in, I also noticed that Kal's nerves became highly excited – they were firing like mad. But the surprising thing was, when he started to slow down his breathing rate, the same nerves began to calm down and a different set started to fire more rapidly. I could see that, as the second set of nerves became more active, his heart rate began to slow down, his body relaxed, even his thoughts were coming at a slower pace. The second set of nerves were obviously more sympathetic to his need to be calm than the first ones."

"I started to pay close attention to what he was doing, to slow his breathing rate down. He began by breathing out the excess air that was in his lungs. Then he breathed in quickly, but softly through his nose, counting one, two, three, four. He let go of his breath straight away – allowing the air to flow out quietly through his nose, counting one, two, three, four, five, six on the out breath. In this way, he was ensuring that his out-breath was longer than his in-breath. I could see that his slowed out-breath was the key to slowing down his heart rate and to calming his overexcited nerves. The length of breaths, he was taking in and letting out was not important – counting to three on the in-breath and five on the out-breath or to five on the in and seven on the out-breath, worked just as well. He allowed a natural pause to happen at the end of the out-breath. Then he breathed in again, counting to four and then out counting to six. He continued breathing in this way, until his whole system had calmed down – it hadn't taken very long. Doing this exercise had even brought about an end to his feeling of shortness of breath.

"It was totally fascinating to watch. However, I would have to say, that it was putting his fearful 'what if' type thoughts on trial, that had brought about the greatest long term benefits for Kal. Using the courtroom scenario, he discovered that his fearful thoughts had no basis in reality – there was no evidence for them out in the real world. With this discovery, an end had been brought about to his sensations of panic — they had in fact disappeared for good.

"But I have gone off on a tangent, so back to my story about how I found my way to you and to this side of the island.

"I had been walking for several hours, when night began to fall and darkness descended on the trail. I could hear faint noises in the distance. I was alone. I didn't know where I was. But I knew now that if the worst happened, I would be able to handle it. The Defense Lawyer had shown me, that I had resources within myself that I hadn't been aware of. I could draw on those, should the need arise. It was true that I was alone and it was dark, but I wasn't unduly worried.

"The next morning when the sun came up, I headed off on my journey again.

"I found that I made the most progress when I followed my instincts. I would say to myself, 'This feels like the right way to go.' Because I wasn't worried and thinking 'What if' this or 'What if' that, I seemed to be able to tune in more to what felt instinctively right.

"And because I wasn't thinking too far ahead, I was able to enjoy all that was going on, right there in the moment. I found myself listening to the different sounds on the trail – the birds twittering and calling to each other. I was seeing things that I had never noticed before. I was enjoying myself."

"It sounds to me, that once you got your thinking on track, then everything else fell into place," Little Brave said.

"Yeah, you are right. That's exactly what happened."

"Would you agree that the biggest challenge that you faced, was the challenge to change yourself?"

"Absolutely."

"You needed to change what was on the inside, before you could make the changes that you needed to make on the outside."

"Yeah, that's it exactly and the great thing was it didn't take long. Once I knew what to do, the changes happened really quickly. Of course it is Weismann that I have to thank for that."

The two friends held up their glasses and said "Here's to Weismann."

It had been a long day and now it was time for bed.

"Good night Little Worrier – I am so glad that you made it."

"Me too, good night, see you in the morning my friend."

Just as he turned over to go to sleep, Little Worrier put his elbow on his pillow and resting his head on it said, "Good night Weismann and thanks again."

But this time there was no reply from Weismann. He had vanished. He had done his job, he wasn't needed anymore and now he had disappeared.

A Training Session in Boston – Part Two

You could have heard a pin drop as Bill finished telling the story. The silence was broken when Dell got to her feet and started to applaud. The others followed.

"You have a great way with words Bill," Abe said.

"Yes I agree," Ann-Marie said. I particularly liked the way that you got into character when you were telling Little Worrier's part of the story."

"Well, I thought it was best to let LW speak for himself," Bill replied. The others laughed.

"I couldn't have told it any better myself," Ann-Marie added, when the laughter had died down.

"OK, it is time now to hear about the lessons that you, yourselves have learned from Little Worrier's story and more importantly, how you have applied those lessons in your own lives. Who would like to get this part of the show on the road?"

Separating Fact from Fiction

"I will give it a go, if you like," Laura said. "Please do," Ann-Marie replied. "My friend Karen had a very bad case of 'what-if-itis,' Laura said. "She was seriously worried about her husband. They have three kids and had been happily married for ten years. But she had started to have doubts about him. 'What if he's having an affair? What if he's going out to meet another woman instead of working late?' She'd gotten herself into a right old state. I told her about Little Worrier's judge and jury. She said 'Let's do it.' When she realized that the Prosecution Lawyer had no real evidence, while the Defense Lawyer had loads of evidence, to prove that he loved her and wasn't having an affair, she was relieved. She realized how crazy she had been and how easy it is to be convinced of something, without having any facts to back it up. Now when either of us says 'What if?' the other one says, 'would you like to go to court?'"

"I have to admit that I have suffered from 'what-if-itis' too," Kurt laughed. "What if the orders don't come in?" "What if business doesn't pick up?" Richard joined in. And together they said "What if we have to let staff go? What if the business goes to the wall?"

"I am able to laugh about it now," Kurt said, "but I can tell you, it wasn't funny at the time. I had many sleepless nights. I couldn't think straight. I couldn't concentrate. I couldn't make a decision to save my life. My head was like mush. Well that's what worry does to you. But doing the judge and jury exercise, really made the difference. Just because you think that something is true and you can see it in your imagination, doesn't mean that it is true – it doesn't mean that it's going to happen; that's the biggest lesson that I took from the story. Anytime, I find myself doing the 'what if' thing now I call in the lawyers. I bring in the judge and the jury. I let them sort it out and the great thing is it doesn't cost me a penny."

"Yeah, but what if it is true? What if you come up with evidence which shows that your 'what ifs' are real? What if the business *is* going to the wall?" Dell asked.

"What does everybody think?" Anne Marie asked. "What happens if you discover that your 'what ifs' are true?"

"Well, if your 'what ifs' are true, then you have a problem on your hands that needs to be solved," Kurt said. "This is a different issue. Now you need to get into problem solving mode. And because you are not running on irrational fear any more, you are in a better place to be able to solve your problem."

"'What if I don't meet someone else,' was a big worry for my sixteen year-old, Jill said. His first real relationship had just ended. I wanted to help him. I tried reassuring him. 'Of course you are going to meet someone else,' I said; 'You are only sixteen years old, for God's sake. You have a lot going for you. You will have lots of relationships.' But he just wasn't taking it in.

"Having read Little Worrier's Story, I suggested that he put his 'what if' on trial. I hoped that this approach would work, where mine had failed. He decided to give it a try. He was very surprised, when he realized that there was in fact no Prosecution evidence — none at all. How could there be? I knew this to be the case, but he needed to find this out for himself.

"Using the lawyer's approach, he also realized that he was overlooking some really important Defense evidence, like the fact that he had many of the qualities that girls look for in a guy; that girls had shown an interest in him in the past and the fact that he'd already had relationships with girls, showed that he had what it took to have relationships in the future. Faced with all of those facts, the only conclusion that he could come to, was that his 'what if' thinking was without foundation and that he was far more likely than not, to have relationships in the future. This approach worked in changing his negative thinking, where my best efforts had failed."

"I think that you are making a really important point here, Jill," Ann-Marie said. "It was doing the Judge and Jury exercise that brought about the change in your son's attitude. In order for that change to come about, he needed to engage in the process of discovering the truth about the situation. As you say, he needed to find out the facts for himself."

"Yes, I agree with you. I could have been pointing out those facts to him, till I was blue in the face and it would have made no difference. He had to see them for himself."

"I can identify with your son, Ellie said. My fear that I wouldn't meet someone new was the reason that I stayed in a relationship that was way past its expiry date. I wasted ten years of my life, because of this fear. Even when I managed to get out of the relationship, this fear – this worry persisted. Putting my 'what if' on trial was the best thing that I ever did. It showed me in a way that nothing else could, that my thinking was 'off the wall'. It is quite extraordinary, just how deluded we can be sometimes. This exercise is worth its weight in gold in getting you to the facts – in moving you beyond delusion, to the reality of a situation."

"I was heading up the organization that I worked for, but my role was purely symbolic." All eyes in the room were now on Ben, as he related his story. "It was a job without substance. I was being well paid for doing very little. And the very little I was doing, held very little interest for me.

"Going into work was a real chore. I had started taking days off. My wife would phone me, just to check that I had gone in. A lot of the time, I was still in bed. Because I wasn't challenging myself in any way, I had started to lose confidence and belief in myself. The thought of going out looking for a new job, brought me out in a cold sweat. I didn't think that I would be able for a new job. I was living in a fur lined mousetrap and I didn't know how to get out of it.

"Then Ann-Marie emailed me about Little Worrier. I read his story and I would have to say, that it was just the ticket that I needed, to get me out of the malaise that I was in.

"Like Little Worrier, I had a very bad dose of the 'what ifs'. 'What if I can't handle a new job? What if I am not able for the pressure? What if I don't get the same money that I am on now?' I could have written a book on the subject. There was nothing for it, but to put my 'what ifs' on trial as he had done.

"The thing that really swung the case in my favor was when the Defense started to go back in time and to bring in evidence of all of the successes and achievements that I'd had in the past – all those times when I had put myself out there and had managed to get myself over the line. There was tons of evidence; my first job after college – I had started on the bottom rung of the ladder – all the hard work that I did – all the experience that I got – all the advances that I made. I had changed tack, half way through my career – all of the difficulties and challenges, that that had brought, that I had faced down and overcome. Going back to do further studies, while working a full time job. I could go on and on.

"This is who I really was – I was a doer – a guy who liked and who could rise to a challenge – not the worrying, under-confident, work shy individual that I believed that I had become. I saw a couple of interesting jobs online the other day. I have sent off my CV. I will keep you posted on how things work out."

Jeff had been listening attentively to what the others were saying. "The company that I worked for was being put through a 'lean process', he said. "They'd brought in consultants to see where cutbacks could be made. They were doing a real root-and-branch job. They had told us that it was necessary, if we were to remain competitive. But we weren't really listening. Everyone was threatened by what it could mean for them. There was a lot of resistance. 'What if they cut my job?' 'What if it's my butt that is on the line?' That's all you heard, day in and day out. Nobody wanted change. They couldn't see any positives in it. Because of all of the hassle, the company decided to close its operation and relocate to Asia. Now we are all out of a job. If only we had read Little Worrier's story, we could have done something about our 'what if's'. If we had, then some of us might still be in a job."

Putting an End to Anxiety

"As I was saying earlier, I went through a bad time with anxiety about six months ago," Josh said. "I was wakening in the morning with tightness across my chest. 'What if it's my heart? What if I'm going to die?' I believed that there was something seriously wrong with me. Nothing could convince me otherwise. I had been to see my doctor. She had assured me that everything was OK. I had gone to see her, several times. She had even sent me for tests at the hospital. They were all clear. They said it was anxiety. But I couldn't get it out of my head. At work, I couldn't concentrate. Every time I got the tight feeling, I thought I was going to drop down dead. I know what Little Worrier means when he says, 'I noticed that when I think frightening thoughts, that my heart beats faster and my breathing speeds up.'

"Well, I put my thoughts on trial as he had done and would you believe it, the only evidence that the Prosecution Lawyer could bring in, to prove the case, was the chest tightness – there was no other evidence. I have to say I smiled. The Defense Lawyer had a field day. He brought in loads of evidence – the doctor visits, the hospital visits, the test results, the non-life threatening explanations that there are for chest tightness, like upper chest rather than diaphragmatic breathing, the length of time I'd had the problem. He won the case hands down. I had been a basket case, yet this simple exercise, had brought home to me the facts about the situation, in a way that I hadn't been able to see before – thank you, Little Worrier."

"I think, that it's important to point out here Josh, that this approach worked for you, because you had gone to your doctor and had been checked out medically, otherwise the Defense Lawyer wouldn't have had the necessary evidence to challenge your 'what if' thinking. Would you agree? Ann-Marie asked."

"Yes definitely," Josh said. "This is what swung the case for me – it was the medical evidence that made the difference."

"'What if I don't meet my targets' was a big worry for me," Jo said. This worry would kick in about the ninth or tenth of each month. Worry has always made me feel anxious. When I am anxious I can't focus. I can't think.

A lot of the time I can't sleep. I didn't really have much faith in the judge and jury thing. I didn't think that it would work for me. But after one particularly bad night, when I hardly slept at all, I decided to give it a go. I figured 'what the hell' – I don't really have anything to lose.

"Unlike, with a lot of other people, the Prosecution Lawyer in my case was able to find evidence in support of my 'what if'. It was the tenth of the month and I still had no orders. To my way of thinking, that was proof, if any were needed, that I had real cause for worry and concern. I could have given up there and then, but as I had started the exercise, I decided to see it through to the end. I was hoping that something might turn up, that would ease my anxiety. Thankfully my hope paid off.

"The Defense Lawyer, when given the opportunity, was able to find several pieces of evidence, which I had previously overlooked and which proved that I was likely to meet my targets. For example, he showed that in the previous nine months, I had managed to meet the targets that I had been given every time. Furthermore, I had secured my first order for each month, but only after the fifteenth day of the month. I still had five days to go. He also showed, that two of the leads that I had, were very good leads, that had borne fruit in the past. It seems hard to believe now, that I hadn't been able to see any of this for myself. The truth is that I had been too worried and too anxious to see it. Worry for me was like a cloud that blocked out the sun. When the worry was there, I couldn't see anything other than the worrying scenario. Using the courtroom exercise, I was able to move beyond worry and into the light of reality."

End Worry – End Anxiety

"I was going to work one morning on the subway, Marissa said. "I felt sick. I thought that I was going to throw up. I had to get off. The next morning, I started feeling really anxious as I got on. Again, I was afraid that I would throw up while in the car. I was so anxious that I had to get off at the next stop. After that, the anxious feeling came over me, every time I went to go on the subway. In time, even thinking about going on the subway made me feel anxious. I tried taking the bus to work – the same thing happened. I couldn't go to work because I couldn't bring myself to go on public transport. This was the stage that I was at, when I read Little Worrier's story.

"There was nothing for it, but to put my 'what if' on trial as he had done. 'What if I get sick while on the subway,' was my biggest worry and the root cause of my anxiety. The Prosecution Lawyer must bring in evidence to prove the case; to prove that I would throw up while I was in transit. Where was the evidence that this was going to happen? I thought about the question and then thought about it some more. To my surprise there was no evidence. Not one shred of evidence. Like Little Worrier, this came as a great relief to me. I had to smile.

"With the Defense Lawyer's help, I realized that of all of the times that I had taken public transport and there had been many – thousands I reckoned, I had never in fact gotten sick while on the subway – not once. Even on the one occasion when I had felt sick and believed that I was going to throw up, I had managed to get out of the car and even then, I hadn't thrown up.

"With the Defense Lawyer's help, I also realized that there had been 'mitigating' circumstances on the day that I believed that I would throw up. I wasn't well. I had a virus, which was making me feel ill. I came to understand, that my sick feeling, was not some random occurrence, that was likely to kick in at just about any time; I was not in fact going to start feeling sick 'out of the blue'. 'What conclusion, would the judge and jury come to, based on the evidence before them?' They would say, that if I wasn't feeling sick before going on the subway, then it was unlikely, that I would start throwing up, while I was on it. This was a big realization for me. With this realization, came freedom – freedom from worry and anxiety. Because I wasn't worried and anxious any more, about throwing up, I was able to go back to using public transport and even more importantly, back to my job. Thank you Little Worrier."

Putting an End to Panic

"I had started having panic attacks, while driving," Julie said. "I was worried, that my car was going to go out of control. I thought that at any moment, it would just veer off the road and hit the barrier or swerve into the inner lane and hit another vehicle.

"While driving in the snow, my car had in fact skidded off the road. This had terrified me. However, I had failed to make the connection between losing control in the snow and my current fear of losing control. I just hadn't seen it. It was the Prosecution Lawyer, who first drew my attention to this connection. She had been looking for evidence, to prove that I would lose control of the car. The evidence that she brought up, was the fact that I had done it before. I had lost control in the snow. Was there any other evidence, which showed that I would now lose control of the car I was driving? I searched for further evidence, but there wasn't any.

"It was time now, to check out the Defense evidence. I had been driving since I was eighteen years old. I am forty five now. I had driven thousands of miles in that time. I thought back over all those times – I thought about all the trips that I had made – long trips and short trips – on wide roads and narrow roads. I thought about all the different cars that I had driven – big cars and not so big cars. In all of that time, I had never lost control of the car that I was driving – not once. This was quite a revelation to me. It showed me, that I was someone who was capable of keeping a car on the road. I also realized that on that one occasion, when I had lost control, there had been a valid reason, why this had happened – the road had been covered in frozen snow. The hazardous road condition was the reason for the car going out of control. The loss of control wasn't some random, 'out of the blue' occurrence that could recur at any time, without warning. The verdict of the judge and jury was obvious – I was not likely to lose control. With this realization, came an end to my panic attacks. How had I not seen this for myself?"

"Sometimes, the hardest thing for us to see is the thing that is right under our own nose," Bill said.

"Yes, you are right Bill," Julie added. "Thinking is a great gift, but it can also be a great curse, when it is allowed to get so out of hand; when it is allowed to go unchecked and unchallenged in this way."

"It sounds to me like you all got something out of reading the book," Ann-Marie said.

"Yeah, I think we took different things from it," Bill said."

Jen, who had been sitting, listening and taking everything in, said, "As I was saying to you earlier, I haven't had a chance to read my copy of the book, because of pressures from work. Now, that I know what to do, I can't wait to put my 'what ifs' on trial. I will keep you posted on how I get on."

"Oh yes, do the judge and jury thing on it Jen, as soon as you can and be done with your worry," the group said, all at the same time.

"I will, in fact I can't wait to do it, now that I have heard your stories."

"I look forward to hearing from you Jen," Ann-Marie said, as she wrapped up the session and thanked the participants, for their feedback.

Bill said, that he believed that everyone would agree with him, that it had been a most interesting and enjoyable day.

Each person said their good byes and told Ann-Marie that they were looking forward very much indeed, to their next meeting.

Thank you for taking the time to read this book. If you have any queries or comments, please contact me at www.bernadettefarrell.com and send me your feedback.

If you are having trouble sleeping, you might like to check out my video *"Help Me Sleep: How to Overcome your Sleep Problems"* at www.bernadettefarrell.com

CPSIA information can be obtained at www.ICGtesting.com
Printed in the USA
LVOW10s1600101215

466281LV00019B/1483/P